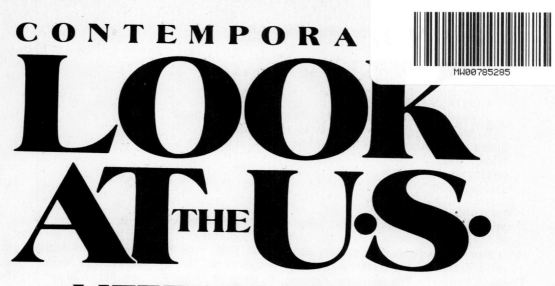

CONTEMPORARY
LOOK
AT THE U·S·
LITERACY LEVEL

SALLY WIGGINTON
Bilingual/ESL
Teacher Training Program Coordinator
Urban Education Program
Associated Colleges of the Midwest
Chicago, Illinois

Project Editor
Kathy Osmus

CONTEMPORARY BOOKS
a division of NTC/CONTEMPORARY PUBLISHING GROUP
Lincolnwood, Illinois USA

Library of Congress Cataloging-in-Publication Data

Wigginton, Sally.
    Look at the U.S. literacy level / Sally Wigginton.
        p.   cm.
    ISBN 0-8092-4329-6
    1. Readers—United States.   2. Readers for new literates.
    3. English language—Textbooks for foreign speakers.   4. United
States—Civilization.   I. Title.   II. Title: Look at the US.
literacy level
    PE1127.H5W54   1989   89-729
    428.6'4—dc19   CIP

Photo credits
Page 1: UPI/Bettmann Newsphotos. Page 11: © Gregg Mancuso/Stock Boston. Page 14a: © Peter Menzel/Stock Boston. Page 14b: H. S. Rice. Courtesy, Department of Library Services, American Museum of Natural History (Negative 312686). Page 14c: The Bettmann Archive, Inc. Page 16: © Michael Philip Manheim/MGA Chicago. Page 17a: Historical Pictures Service, Chicago. Page 17b: The Bettmann Archive, Inc. Page 19: Culver Pictures. Pages 20 and 21: The Bettmann Archive, Inc. Page 22: Courtesy The Library of Congress. Page 24: © Susan Malis/ MGA Chicago. Page 25: UPI/Bettmann Newsphotos. Page 27: Historical Pictures Service, Chicago. Pages 29 and 31: UPI/Bettmann Newsphotos. Page 32: AP/Wide World Photos. Pages 35 and 37: UPI/Bettmann Newsphotos. Page 38: © Billy E. Barnes/Stock Boston. Page 40: © Burt Glinn/Magnum Photos. Pages 43 and 45: UPI/Bettmann Newsphotos.

ISBN: 0-8092-4329-6

Published by Contemporary Books,
a division of NTC/Contemporary Publishing Group, Inc.,
4255 West Touhy Avenue,
Lincolnwood (Chicago), Illinois 60646-1975 U.S.A.

8 9 0 C(K) 13 12 11 10 9 8

Editorial Director Caren Van Slyke	*Illustrators* Rosemary Morrissey-Herzberg Guy Wolek
Editorial Julie Landau Lisa Dillman Lynn McEwan Pat Coyne	*Photo Researcher* Julie Laffin
	Art & Production Princess Louise El Andrea Haracz Jan Geist
Editorial/Production Manager Patricia Reid	
Production Editor Craig Bolt	*Typography* Carol Schoder
Cover Design Lois Koehler	Cover photo © The Image Bank Photographer: Guido Albert Rossi

Contents

To the Instructor

This book in the *Look at the U.S.* series was specifically designed for both preliterate and beginning-level ESL students. With this text, you can introduce the basics of American history and government to students who are able to read little or no English.

A Personal Approach

The book is divided into three sections:

- The first, "America and Its People," reinforces personal identification information. It also orients students to local, national, and global perspectives and teaches basic map skills.

- The second section, "American History Through Holidays," provides information on key people and events. The lessons provide historical background and are presented in the context of American holidays that students may be familiar with.

- The third section, "American Government," introduces basic government structures and laws. These lessons are informative and linked to students' daily lives.

Instructional Design

Each chapter has two pages. The left-hand page is pictorially based, combining speaking and listening skills with an activity-based exercise (circling, matching, etc.) Thus, students who read no English at all can be directed through these pages.

The right-hand page of each chapter is designed for the low-beginning student. It contains a picture and a brief content passage. This passage may be used for listening or reading comprehension, depending on students' abilities. The exercises that follow are brief and can be conducted as class or individual work. Students at this level may also enjoy the activity on the left-hand page of the lesson.

Thus, this two-level lesson format allows you the flexibility to use part or all of the materials with your class.

Pictures and Print

Even though many of your students will not be able to read, the presence of English words will not inhibit their use of the materials. The lessons have been designed so that they can be used exclusively for speaking and listening if necessary. (In some cases, individual sight words are presented with picture cues.) By familiarizing students with materials containing print, you are preparing them for the next stage in their learning.

The *Look at the U.S.* Series

There is a special teacher's guide to accompany this text—*Literacy Level Teacher's Guide* (ISBN: 0-8092-4328-8). The guide provides additional ideas for step-by-step instruction of the core materials. The guide also presents dozens of additional classroom extension activities to reinforce content or provide a life-skills focus to the materials.

For students at higher levels of English proficiency, there are two more books in this series. For more information on the entire series, contact:

Contemporary Books, a division of NTC/Contemporary Publishing Company, 4255 West Touhy Avenue, Lincolnwood (Chicago), Illinois, 60646-1975, U.S.A.

Out toll-free number is (800) 621-1918.

Content-Based ESL

Presenting content-area material, such as history and government, may be a new experience for many ESL instructors. It is an especially challenging task for instructors working with students who are at very low levels of English proficiency. However, you have many factors working in your favor.

Your key advantage is the students themselves. They are very motivated to learn more about the United States. This text will put the life-coping skills that students are learning into the broader context of American society.

Another important factor is your own expertise. Some ESL instructors are already teaching many of the issues covered in this text, such as personal identification, the calendar, and important holidays. This text provides a framework for these ideas—a framework that will allow you to conform to INS amnesty guidelines.

Finally, the format and content of this book works to your advantage. The abundance of pictures and the small amount of text allow students at even the lowest levels of English proficiency to grasp key concepts. The amount of concepts has been carefully controlled so that students at these levels will not be overwhelmed. At the same time, the personalized focus of the book will allow students to relate to the materials.

We hope that the use of *Look at the U.S.—Literacy Level* will make the teaching and learning process easy and enjoyable for all concerned.

America and Its People

The people of America come from many different countries.

Chapter 1
My Story

Listen and Repeat

My name is Monica Gonzales.

My address is 127 W. Monroe Street.

I live in Chicago, Illinois.

Listen and Answer

1. What is your name? My name is _____.

2. What is your address? My address is _____.

3. Where do you live? I live in _____, _____.
   _____(city)_____ _____(state)_____

TEACHER'S NOTE: Use the pictures to reinforce the concepts of "address," "street" (avenue, road, etc.), "city," and "state" (the focus of the next lesson). Explain the "W." in W. Monroe.

Learn About
Monica

My name is Monica Gonzales.

I live in Chicago, Illinois.

My address is 127 W. Monroe Street.

I am 23 years old and married.

I am from Rodeo, Durango.

The state of Durango is in the country of Mexico.

Write About Monica

Name: _____
    (Last)   (First)

Address: _____
    (Number)   (Street)

_____
    (City)   (State)

Sex: Male __ Female __   Age: ___

Signature: _____

Write About Yourself

Name: _____
    (Last)   (First)   (Middle)

Address: _____
    (Number)   (Street)

_____
    (City)   (State)   (Zip Code)

Sex: Male __ Female __   Age: ___

Signature: _____

TEACHER'S NOTE: First, use information about yourself as an example. It may also be necessary to demonstrate the difference between the concepts of "name" and "signature." Explain the "W." in W. Monroe.

Chapter 2
In the U.S.

Listen and Repeat

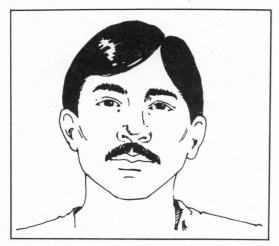

I am Carlos Sanchez.

I live in Sacramento, California.

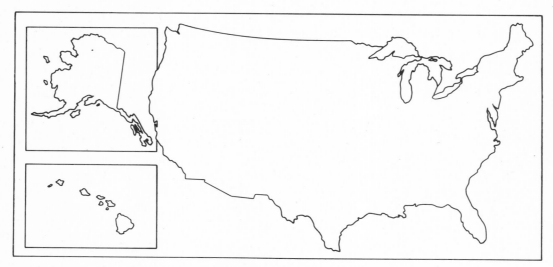

I live in the United States.

Listen and Answer

1. What city do you live in? I live in _____.

2. What state do you live in? I live in _____.

3. Point to your state on the map of the U.S. on page 5.

4. What country do you live in? I live in _____.

TEACHER'S NOTE: First, familiarize students with the U.S. map. Then use the pictures to illustrate the differences between "city," "state," and "country."

Learn About
the United States

The leaders of a country work in the capital city. The capital of the whole United States is Washington, D.C.

There are 50 states in the United States. Each state in the U.S. also has a capital city.

This map shows Washington, D.C., and the 50 states.

Listen and Answer

1. What is the capital of the U.S.?

2. What state do you live in?

3. What is the capital of your state?

4. Name a state in the East.

5. Name a state in the West.

6. Is your native country divided into states?

7. What is the capital of your native country?

TEACHER'S NOTE: Use the map on this page to illustrate the concepts of "state" and the "capital" of a country. Also, explain the concept of "north," "south," "east," and "west."

Chapter 3
In the World

Listen and Repeat

My name is Merilee LaRue.

I am from Port-au-Prince.
Port-au-Prince is a large city in
Haiti.

Haiti is a small country.
Haiti is on an island near the
United States.

Listen and Do

1. Find Haiti on the large map. Circle it.

2. Find the United States. Put an X on it.

3. Find the Atlantic Ocean. Put a □ on it.

4. Find the Gulf of Mexico. Put a △ on it.

TEACHER'S NOTE: Make sure the concepts of "city," "country," and "island" are clear.
Use examples to show the differences between "large," "small," "near," and "far."

Learn About the World

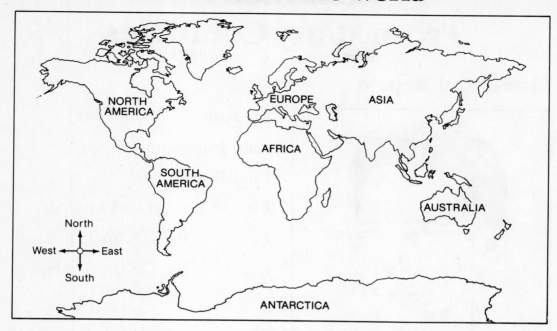

There are 7 continents in the world. A continent is a large area of land. The United States is on the continent of North America.

Listen and Answer

1. What country are you from? I am from _____.

2. What continent is your native country on? My native country

   is on the continent of _____.

Look at a World Map

1. Name 2 countries in North America.

2. Name 2 countries in South America.

3. Name 2 countries in Europe.

4. Name 2 countries in Africa.

5. Name 2 countries in Asia.

TEACHER'S NOTE: First, go over the continents on the map on this page. Then have students refer to the world map on pages 48 and 49 to answer the last five questions.

Chapter 4
From Many Countries

Listen and Repeat

My name is Young Cho.

I am from South Korea.

I am Korean.

I speak Korean and English.

I came to the U.S. in 1976.

I came to the U.S. by airplane.

1. Where are you from? I am from _____.
2. What is your nationality? I am _____.
3. What languages do you speak? I speak _____ and English.
4. When did you come to the U.S.? I came to the U.S. in _____.
5. How did you come to the U.S.? I came to the U.S. by _____.

Show How People Came to the U.S.

Name	Airplane	Boat	Bus	Foot	Other ?
Young Cho	X				

TEACHER'S NOTE: Make the distinction between "country" and "nationality" by example—*America-American, Vietnam-Vietnamese*, etc. Be sure students understand the chart.

Learn About These People

I am Bill Nikos.

I am from Greece.

I am Greek.

I speak Greek and English.

I came to the U.S. in 1908.

I am Stefania Kroll.

I am from Poland.

I am Polish.

I speak Polish and English.

I came to the U.S. in 1982.

Write About Yourself and Copy the Sentences

1. I am from _____.
   (country)

   _____

2. I am _____.
   (nationality)

   _____

3. I speak _____ and English.
   (language)

   _____

4. I came to the U.S. in _____.
   (year)

   _____

TEACHER'S NOTE: First, present your own personal information as an example. Then do this exercise orally before having students write.

American History Through Holidays

We celebrate American history with holidays.

Chapter 5
The Calendar

Learn the Months of the Year

January	February	March	April
S M T W T F S	S M T W T F S	S M T W T F S	S M T W T F S
1 2 3 4 5 6 7	1 2 3 4	1 2 3 4	1
8 9 10 11 12 13 14	5 6 7 8 9 10 11	5 6 7 8 9 10 11	2 3 4 5 6 7 8
15 16 17 18 19 20 21	12 13 14 15 16 17 18	12 13 14 15 16 17 18	9 10 11 12 13 14 15
22 23 24 25 26 27 28	19 20 21 22 23 24 25	19 20 21 22 23 24 25	16 17 18 19 20 21 22
29 30 31	26 27 28	26 27 28 29 30 31	23 24 25 26 27 28 29
			30

May	June	July	August
S M T W T F S	S M T W T F S	S M T W T F S	S M T W T F S
1 2 3 4 5 6	1 2 3	1	1 2 3 4 5
7 8 9 10 11 12 13	4 5 6 7 8 9 10	2 3 4 5 6 7 8	6 7 8 9 10 11 12
14 15 16 17 18 19 20	11 12 13 14 15 16 17	9 10 11 12 13 14 15	13 14 15 16 17 18 19
21 22 23 24 25 26 27	18 19 20 21 22 23 24	16 17 18 19 20 21 22	20 21 22 23 24 25 26
28 29 30 31	25 26 27 28 29 30	23 24 25 26 27 28 29	27 28 29 30 31
		30 31	

September	October	November	December
S M T W T F S	S M T W T F S	S M T W T F S	S M T W T F S
1 2	1 2 3 4 5 6 7	1 2 3 4	1 2
3 4 5 6 7 8 9	8 9 10 11 12 13 14	5 6 7 8 9 10 11	3 4 5 6 7 8 9
10 11 12 13 14 15 16	15 16 17 18 19 20 21	12 13 14 15 16 17 18	10 11 12 13 14 15 16
17 18 19 20 21 22 23	22 23 24 25 26 27 28	19 20 21 22 23 24 25	17 18 19 20 21 22 23
24 25 26 27 28 29 30	29 30 31	26 27 28 29 30	24 25 26 27 28 29 30
			31

1. How many months are in a year?

   There are _____ months in a year.

2. Repeat the names of the months.

   The months are _____ .

3. Match the Months

Jan.	November
Feb.	September
Sept.	January
Nov.	December
Dec.	February

Learn the Days of the Week

AUGUST						
Sunday	Monday	Tuesday	Wednesday	Thursday	Friday	Saturday
		1	2	3	4	5
6	7	8	9	10	11	12

1. How many days are in a week? There are _____ days in a week.

2. Name the days of the week. The days of the week are _____ .

TEACHER'S NOTE: Students should be encouraged to learn the days and months in order and as sight words. Students' personal dates such as birthdays and anniversaries may also be circled on the calendar.

Learn About the Holidays

In the United States, we celebrate many holidays. Holidays are special days to remember important people and events in our history.

In your native country, what special holidays do you celebrate? What new holidays have you celebrated in the U.S.?

Listen and Do

Circle the third Monday in January. This is Martin Luther King, Jr., Day.

January						
S	M	T	W	T	F	S
1	2	3	4	5	6	7
8	9	10	11	12	13	14
15	16	17	18	19	20	21
22	23	24	25	26	27	28
29	30	31				

Circle February 12. This is Lincoln's Birthday.
Circle February 22. This is Washington's Birthday.

February						
S	M	T	W	T	F	S
			1	2	3	4
5	6	7	8	9	10	11
12	13	14	15	16	17	18
19	20	21	22	23	24	25
26	27	28				

Circle the last Monday in May. This is Memorial Day.

May						
S	M	T	W	T	F	S
	1	2	3	4	5	6
7	8	9	10	11	12	13
14	15	16	17	18	19	20
21	22	23	24	25	26	27
28	29	30	31			

Circle July 4. This is Independence Day.

July						
S	M	T	W	T	F	S
						1
2	3	4	5	6	7	8
9	10	11	12	13	14	15
16	17	18	19	20	21	22
23	24	25	26	27	28	29
30	31					

Circle the first Monday in September. This is Labor Day.

September						
S	M	T	W	T	F	S
					1	2
3	4	5	6	7	8	9
10	11	12	13	14	15	16
17	18	19	20	21	22	23
24	25	26	27	28	29	30

Circle the second Monday in October. This is Columbus Day.

October						
S	M	T	W	T	F	S
1	2	3	4	5	6	7
8	9	10	11	12	13	14
15	16	17	18	19	20	21
22	23	24	25	26	27	28
29	30	31				

Circle the fourth Thursday of November. This is Thanksgiving Day.

November						
S	M	T	W	T	F	S
			1	2	3	4
5	6	7	8	9	10	11
12	13	14	15	16	17	18
19	20	21	22	23	24	25
26	27	28	29	30		

TEACHER'S NOTE: Distinguish between expressions such as "February 12" and "the third Monday in January." Use the list of cardinal and ordinal numbers on page 47 to help with dates.

October
S M T W T F S
1 2 3 4 5 6 7
8 9 10 11 12 13 14
15 16 17 18 19 20 21
22 23 24 25 26 27 28
29 30 31

Chapter 6
Columbus Day

Match the Pictures and the Sentences

1. American Indians were living in America.

2. Christopher Columbus landed in America in 1492.

3. On the second Monday in October, we celebrate Columbus Day with parades.

___

___

___

TEACHER'S NOTE: First, read or summarize the story of Columbus on page 15 and answer students' questions. Then read the sentences above, one at a time. Have students write the number of the sentence beneath the corresponding picture.

Learn About
Christopher Columbus

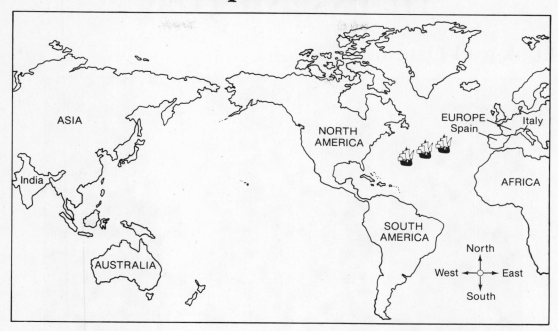

Christopher Columbus was an Italian explorer.	Put an X on Italy.
He wanted to go to India.	Put a ✓ on India.
He got money and boats from the Queen of Spain.	Put a △ on Spain.
Columbus and his men sailed in 3 boats.	Circle the 3 boats.
In 1492, Columbus landed in North America. He thought he was in India.	Put a ☐ on North America.
There were people already living on the land. Columbus called the people Indians.	Draw a line from Spain to North America.

TEACHER'S NOTE: After the story and activity are combined, the story may be read in its entirety by covering the right-hand column.

15

November
S M T W T F S
            1 2 3 4
5 6 7 8 9 10 11
12 13 14 15 16 17 18
19 20 21 22 (23) 24 25
26 27 28 29 30

Chapter 7
Thanksgiving Day

Look and Listen

Americans celebrate Thanksgiving to give thanks for family, friends, food, and health.

Circle Your Answer

1. In what season did you come to the U.S.?

winter   spring   summer   fall

2. Where did you live when you came to the U.S.?

a house   an apartment   a church

TEACHER'S NOTE: Before doing the exercises, summarize the story about the Pilgrims on page 17 to the students. Introduce new words using the pictures and labels.

Learn About the Pilgrims

In 1620, the Pilgrims came to America from England. They came in the winter. They were cold and hungry.

The Indians helped them find food and build homes. In the fall, the Pilgrims and the Indians had a big feast. They gave thanks for the food. This was the first Thanksgiving.

Listen and Answer

1. What are special holidays in your native country?

2. What do these holidays celebrate?

3. What special foods do you eat on these holidays?

4. What do you do on Thanksgiving Day in the United States?

5. Have you ever been to an American Thanksgiving dinner?

TEACHER'S NOTE: Be sure to discuss each picture in detail. Refer students to the picture of a modern Thanksgiving on page 16.

July						
S	M	T	W	T	F	S
						1
2	3	④	5	6	7	8
9	10	11	12	13	14	15
16	17	18	19	20	21	22
23	24	25	26	27	28	29
30	31					

Chapter 8
The Fourth of July

Listen and Answer

The Fourth of July is a holiday that celebrates America's independence from England.

1. Does your country celebrate an independence day?

2. How do you celebrate it?

3. Do you celebrate the Fourth of July?

4. Circle how you celebrate the Fourth of July.

picnic

fireworks

parade

barbecue

TEACHER'S NOTE: Use concrete examples of personal and political independence to aid students. Again, introduce new words by using the pictures and labels.

Learn About
American Independence

    The Fourth of July is an important holiday in the U.S. We call this holiday Independence Day to celebrate our freedom.

    In 1776, England had 13 colonies in America. The American colonies were not free. The colonists wrote the Declaration of Independence to tell England that they wanted to be free.

    The colonies fought a war against England. This war was called the American Revolution. The colonies won and became the United States of America in 1783.

✔ Check Yes or No

1. The American Revolution was fought against Spain.   Yes ☐ No ☐

2. We celebrate the Fourth of July to remember U.S. independence.   Yes ☐ No ☐

3. My native country celebrates an independence day.   Yes ☐ No ☐

TEACHER'S NOTE: Before beginning the reading, explain that the picture shows soldiers fighting in the American Revolution.

February
S M T W T F S
            1 2 3 4
5 6 7 8 9 10 11
12 13 14 15 16 17 18
19 20 21 (22) 23 24 25
26 27 28

Chapter 9
George Washington's Birthday

Look and Listen

George Washington was the first president of the United States.

Washington's Birthday is on February 22.

George Washington was called "The Father of His Country." We remember him in many ways.

Circle the Memorials to Washington

1.

2.  California    Illinois    Washington

3. dime   quarter   penny

TEACHER'S NOTE: Discuss each picture before students do the activity. Explain that some states observe Presidents' Day.

Learn About the
First President

We celebrate George Washington's birthday on February 22. The picture shows Washington as the leader of the army in the American Revolution. The American colonies won the war. They became independent from England.

The new country called itself the United States of America. A new government was started. George Washington was elected the first U.S. president in 1789. He helped begin the United States.

Fill in the Timeline

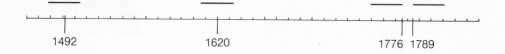

1492   1620   1776 1789

1. The Declaration of Independence was written.

2. Columbus came to America.

3. George Washington was elected president.

4. The first Thanksgiving was celebrated.

TEACHER'S NOTE: First, review information in previous chapters before working with the timeline. Then have the students write the number of the corresponding sentence above the correct year.

February
S M T W T F S
1 2 3 4
5 6 7 8 9 10 11
12 13 14 15 16 17 18
19 20 21 22 23 24 25
26 27 28

Chapter 10
Abraham Lincoln's Birthday

Look and Listen

Abraham Lincoln was the sixteenth president of the United States.

He kept the U.S. together as 1 country.

Lincoln's Birthday is on February 12.

Match the Picture of Lincoln and the Word

1. stamp

2. penny

3. $5 bill

TEACHER'S NOTE: Read or summarize the story of the Civil War on page 23 to explain what is meant by "He kept the U.S. together as 1 country."

Learn About the Civil War

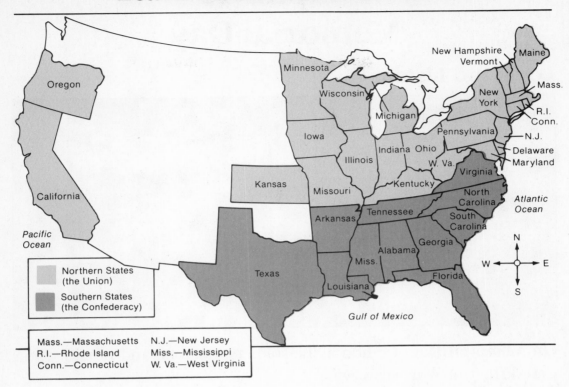

Northern States (the Union)
Southern States (the Confederacy)

Mass.—Massachusetts   N.J.—New Jersey
R.I.—Rhode Island   Miss.—Mississippi
Conn.—Connecticut   W. Va.—West Virginia

We celebrate Abraham Lincoln's birthday on February 12. Lincoln was the sixteenth U.S. president.

Lincoln was president during the Civil War. The U.S. was split into the North and the South. There were 2 reasons for the war: money and slavery. Lincoln brought the U.S. together again.

The Civil War lasted from 1861 to 1865. In 1865 the North won the war. One angry man shot and killed Lincoln.

Write the Following

1. 3 states in the North: _____, _____,

   and _____

2. 3 states in the South: _____, _____,

   and _____

TEACHER'S NOTE: Use the map and its key on this page to explain the concept of the U.S. separating into two countries.

23

May
S M T W T F S
        1 2 3 4 5 6
7 8 9 10 11 12 13
14 15 16 17 18 19 20
21 22 23 24 25 26 27
28 (29) 30 31

Chapter 11
Memorial Day

Look and Listen

On Memorial Day, we honor the soldiers, doctors, and nurses who were killed in American wars.

Listen and Match

1. On Memorial Day, many people do not have to work.

2. Some people visit the graves of loved ones.

3. Some people visit memorials.

TEACHER'S NOTE: Go over the words "soldiers," "doctors," "nurses," "graves," and "memorials." Discuss each picture before beginning the matching exercise.

Learn About
the Wars

In the 1900s, the U.S. fought in 4 major wars. Many American men and women were killed. We honor these men and women on Memorial Day.

Many people do not work on Memorial Day. On that day, they remember the people who were injured or killed. Some people remember with parades. Others remember by visiting the graves of soldiers.

World War I	World War II	Korean War	Vietnam War
1914–1918	1939–1945	1950–1953	1954–1975

Circle Yes or No

1. In the 1900s, the U.S. fought in only 1 war.   Yes   No

2. Many people were killed in the wars.   Yes   No

3. On Memorial Day, we honor people who were   Yes   No
   injured or killed in wars.

4. Only men were killed in the wars.   Yes   No

TEACHER'S NOTE: Explain that the picture shows a memorial parade for soldiers. Also, go over each war on the timeline before beginning the exercise.

Chapter 12
Labor Day

Listen and Answer

factory

office

restaurant

Labor Day is a national holiday to honor workers.
On Labor Day, most people do not have to work.

1. What is your job?

2. Name 2 good things about your job. Name 2 bad things.

Match the Hat with the Workplace

chef's hat

hard hat

nurse's hat

hospital

restaurant

construction

TEACHER'S NOTE: Discuss all of the pictures of the workplaces at the top of the page.
Also, go over the pictures in the matching activity before you start.

Learn About
Labor Day

On Labor Day we celebrate the workers of America. We do this with parades, barbecues, and picnics. Labor Day has been a national holiday since 1894.

Look at the picture of people working in the 1800s. Work was very hard then. Some people worked 15 to 16 hours a day. Many people worked 6 or 7 days a week. Women and children worked for very little money.

Some workers wanted to stop these problems. They got together in unions. The unions helped the people to make their jobs better.

Circle the Things That Help Workers

1. 18-hour workdays   8-hour workdays

2. more money   less money

3. health insurance   no health insurance

4. dangerous workplace   safe workplace

TEACHER'S NOTE: Go over all of the terms before starting the exercise. The concepts of "health insurance" and "dangerous workplace" may be especially challenging. Examples from students' own jobs should prove helpful.

January
S M T W T F S
1 2 3 4 5 6 7
8 9 10 11 12 13 14
15 16 17 18 19 20 21
22 23 24 25 26 27 28
29 30 31

Chapter 13
Martin Luther King, Jr.,
Day

Match the Words and Pictures

1. school   2. vote   3. work   4. home

Listen and Answer

1. Martin Luther King, Jr., believed in good schools for everyone.
   - What do you like about school?

2. Martin Luther King, Jr., believed in good jobs for everyone.
   - Do you have a job?
   - Is it a good job?

3. Martin Luther King, Jr., believed in good homes for everyone.
   - Where do you live?
   - Is it a good place to live?

4. Martin Luther King, Jr., believed that everyone should vote.
   - Would you like to vote in the U.S.?

TEACHER'S NOTE: Go over the pictures and words before starting the matching activity. Follow up the questions with specific examples from students' lives.

Learn About
the Civil Rights Movement

Martin Luther King, Jr., was a leader of the civil rights movement. The people in the civil rights movement wanted everyone to have equal rights in education, housing, jobs, and voting.

Martin Luther King, Jr., and other people worked very hard for these rights. They worked together for peaceful change. The picture shows King and others marching for change.

In 1968, Martin Luther King, Jr., was shot and killed. We celebrate his birthday to remember his work in civil rights.

Copy the Slogans Under the Headings

| HIRE MORE MINORITIES! | REGISTER TO VOTE! | DON'T RAISE OUR RENT! | MORE TEACHERS! |

Schools

_____

Work

_____

Housing

_____

Voting

_____

TEACHER'S NOTE: Discuss the photo of the civil rights march and what it shows. Be sure to explain the slogans and how to do the exercise. You can use this chapter to have students talk about changes in society they would like to see.

American Government

The government protects and serves the people.

Chapter 14
Important People to Know

Listen and Choose

state

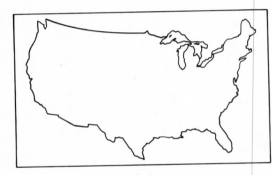

United States

city

1. The president is the leader of the _____.

2. The governor is the leader of the _____.

3. The mayor is the leader of the _____.

Listen and Answer

1. This is the president of the United States. What is his name?

2. Who is the governor of your state?

3. Who is the mayor of your city?

TEACHER'S NOTE: Go over the pictures before starting the matching exercise. Also, ask the students about their community leaders. These can include religious leaders, business leaders, or activists.

Learn About
Important People and Places

White House

State Capitol Building

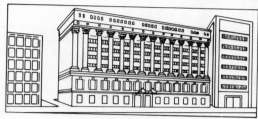
City Hall

The president of the United States is Bill Clinton. He lives and works in the White House in Washington, D.C. The vice president is Al Gore.

Every state has a governor. The governor works in the city that is the state capital. Who is the governor of your state?

Cities and towns have mayors. A mayor works in the city hall. Who is the mayor of your city?

Find the Words

D	C	A	P	I	T	A	L	W	A	B
T	I	S	T	O	P	S	T	O	P	S
M	T	M	A	Y	O	R	S	L	O	V
A	Y	T	L	Y	V	S	G	Y	D	D
W	H	I	T	E	H	O	U	S	E	X
B	A	P	R	E	S	I	D	E	N	T
X	L	H	S	T	A	T	E	J	H	V
X	L	G	O	V	E	R	N	O	R	G

CAPITAL
CITY HALL
GOVERNOR
MAYOR
PRESIDENT
STATE
WHITE HOUSE

TEACHER'S NOTE: Go over the pictures at the top of the page before starting the reading. Demonstrate how to do a word find before starting the activity. Explain to the students that the answers go across and up and down.

Chapter 15
Obeying the Laws

Listen and Circle the Picture

Everyone must obey the laws.
Laws are made to help the government and to protect people.

1. We pay sales taxes to the state. This money is used to build roads and schools.

 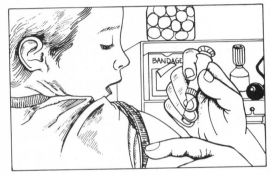

2. We obey driving laws to protect people's safety.

3. Children must get shots before they go to school. The shots protect children so they do not get sick.

 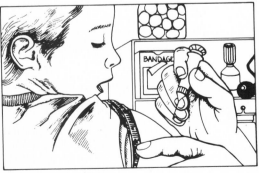

TEACHER'S NOTE: Go over each picture before starting the exercise. Also, encourage students to talk about other laws that they encounter.

Learn About
Obeying the Laws

Some laws help the government to work. For example, we pay sales taxes on what we buy in a restaurant or store. The taxes are used to pay for new roads and schools.

Other laws are also made to protect people. There are traffic laws that set speed limits. These speed limits help to prevent accidents.

There are also special laws to protect children. Children must have certain shots before they can go to school. When they have the shots, children do not catch or pass along some diseases.

Think and Answer

1. What would happen if no one paid taxes?

2. Do laws against speeding do any good? Why or why not?

3. What would happen if children did not get their shots?

TEACHER'S NOTE: Refer to the pictures on page 34 to illustrate the different types of laws discussed in the passage. Also, use the picture at the top of this page to illustrate the consequences of not obeying certain driving laws such as speed limits and stop signs.

Chapter 16
Making the Laws

Listen and Match

There are three levels of government.

There is the U.S. government, the state government, and the city government.

They all make different laws.

___

___

___

1. The U.S. government makes laws about citizenship.

2. The state government makes laws about marriage and divorce.

3. The city government makes laws that the police enforce.

TEACHER'S NOTE: Read the sentences to the students. Then discuss what each picture shows before reading the sentences again. Have students match each sentence with the corresponding picture.

Learn About
Where the Laws Are Made

Laws that are made for the whole United States are called federal laws. The U.S. Congress in Washington, D.C., makes federal laws. The U.S. Congress is made up of two parts: the Senate and the House of Representatives.

Each state has a legislature that is elected to make state laws. Most state legislatures have both a state senate and state house of representatives.

A city council or village board makes local laws.

Circle Yes or No

1. Federal laws are made by the U.S. Congress.   Yes   No

2. State laws are made by the U.S. Congress.   Yes   No

3. Every state has both a senate and a house of   Yes   No
   representatives.

4. Local laws are made by city councils or village   Yes   No
   boards.

TEACHER'S NOTE: Tell students that the picture shows the U.S. Capitol building, where federal laws are made. Be sure to review the words "every" and "most" before starting the exercise.

Chapter 17
The Courts

Look and Listen

This is a courtroom.

In a courtroom, a judge or jury decides if a law has been broken.

If people are found guilty of a crime, they are punished.

Look at the Picture

1. Find the letter A. This is a lawyer.

2. Find the letter B. This is a judge.

3. Find the letter C. This is a jury.

4. Find the letter D. This is a witness.

Listen and Answer

1. What are some laws in your community?

2. Have you ever gotten a ticket? What was it for?

3. Have you ever been to court? Talk about it.

TEACHER'S NOTE: When finding the lawyer, judge, jury, and witness in the picture, describe to students what each one does.

Learn About the Constitution

The Supreme Court

The Constitution is the basic law of the United States. It was written in 1787. We have many other laws to protect the country and its people. All laws must agree with the Constitution.

The most important court in the United States is the Supreme Court. The 9 judges of the Supreme Court decide if laws agree with the Constitution. There are also other kinds of courts in the U.S. For example, there are traffic courts and criminal courts.

Listen and Answer

1. The minimum wage is $3.35 an hour. Mr. Smith hires José for $3.00 an hour. Who is breaking the law? What might happen?

2. The speed limit is 55 miles per hour. Ann is driving at 67 miles per hour. Is Ann breaking the law? What might happen?

3. The Constitution gives people the right to freedom of speech. Mayor James tries to stop the Equal Rights Group from having a meeting. Who is breaking the law? What might happen?

TEACHER'S NOTE: Go over the questions slowly. Be sure to define terms such as "minimum wage," "speed limit," and "freedom of speech."

Chapter 18
Voting

Look and Listen

Citizens of the United States have the right to vote.

People can vote if they are:

- 18 years old or older
- citizens of the United States
- registered to vote
- residents of their state for at least 30 days

Circle What You Would Vote For

guns   no guns   smoking   no smoking

Clinton   Dole

TEACHER'S NOTE: Discuss each pair of opposites before starting the circling activity. Explain that Bill Clinton and Bob Dole were presidential candidates in 1996.

Learn About Voting Laws

U.S. Constitution	Amendment 15	Amendment 19	Amendment 26
1789	1870	1920	1971
White men 21 years old or older could vote.	Black men could vote.	Women could vote.	The voting age was lowered to 18.

When the United States was started, only white men could vote. This was not fair, so the Constitution was changed. Because of the changes, all adults 18 years old or older can vote. This includes whites and nonwhites, men and women.

During the 1960s, special laws were made to help people to vote. One new law was made so that people did not have to pay to vote. This helped poor people. Another law was made so that people could vote even if they could not read very well. Now all of these people have the right to vote.

✔ Check Yes or No

1. Only men can vote.   Yes ☐ No ☐

2. People who are 18 years old can vote.   Yes ☐ No ☐

3. Only rich people can vote.   Yes ☐ No ☐

4. Since the Constitution was changed, more   Yes ☐ No ☐
   people can vote.

TEACHER'S NOTE: Go over the timeline of amendments at the top of the page to explain how voting laws have changed. Be sure to explain the word "only" before starting the exercise.

41

Chapter 19
American Symbols

Match the Symbol and the Words

These symbols represent the United States and its history.

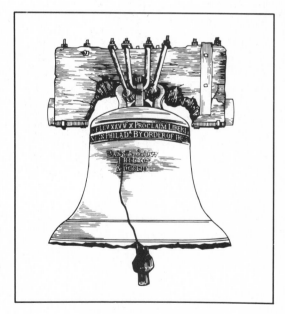

_____ American flag

_____ Statue of Liberty

_____ Liberty Bell

1. Pledge of Allegiance and freedom

2. The American Revolution and independence

3. Welcoming immigrants to the U.S.

TEACHER'S NOTE: Discuss each symbol before starting the matching activity. Explain to students where each of these symbols can be seen.

Learn About
American Symbols

    The picture shows the Statue of Liberty. It is a symbol of political freedom and opportunity for immigrants. It is also a symbol of world friendship. The statue welcomes many people who come to America to start a new life. It is in New York City, New York.

    The American flag is the symbol for freedom in the U.S. The flag is red, white, and blue. The 13 stripes represent the first 13 colonies. The 50 stars represent the 50 states.

    The Liberty Bell is a symbol of the American Revolution. On July 4, 1776, the bell rang when the Declaration of Independence was signed. The Liberty Bell is in Philadelphia, Pennsylvania.

Answer the Questions

1. What does the Statue of Liberty mean to new immigrants to America?

2. Where have you seen the American flag?

3. Where can you see the Liberty Bell?

TEACHER'S NOTE: Use the pictures on page 42 to illustrate the three symbols. Have students discuss some symbols of their native countries.

Chapter 20
Permanent Residency and Citizenship

Look and Listen

My name is Katrina Amado. I am a permanent resident of the United States. I am a citizen of my native country, Guatemala. I hope to return to Guatemala some day to see my family. As a permanent resident, I can live and work in the U.S.

My name is Jan Solasky. I am from Poland. I am a naturalized citizen of the United States. I brought my family to the U.S. last year. I wanted them to become U.S. citizens, too. As a citizen, I can live, work, and vote in the U.S. My family can live here, too.

Listen and Circle Yes or No

1. A permanent resident can vote.   Yes   No

2. A naturalized citizen can bring his or her family to the U.S.   Yes   No

3. A permanent resident can remain a citizen of his or her native country.   Yes   No

4. A naturalized citizen is born in the U.S.   Yes   No

TEACHER'S NOTE: Before beginning the activity, make sure that students are clear on the differences between permanent residency and citizenship.

Learn About
Becoming a U.S. Citizen

Requirements for Becoming a Citizen

To become a naturalized citizen, a person must:

- be at least 18 years old
- have lived in the U.S. as a legal resident for at least 5 years (3 years if the person is married to a U.S. citizen)
- be able to read, write, speak, and understand basic English
- have a basic knowledge and understanding of the history, government structure, and the Constitution of the U.S.
- be willing to take an oath of allegiance to the U.S.

Answer the Questions

Practice asking and answering these questions with another student.

1. Who was the first U.S. president?

2. Who was Abraham Lincoln?

3. Who is the U.S. president now?

4. Who is the governor of your state?

5. What is the capital of your state?

6. Describe the American flag.

TEACHER'S NOTE: Use this activity to refresh students' memories about some basic issues in American history and government.

Appendix 1

Holidays

1998

Months

January

February

March

April

May

June

July

August

September

October

November

December

Days of the Week

Sunday (Su)

Monday (M)

Tuesday (Tu)

Wednesday (W)

Thursday (Th)

Friday (F)

Saturday (Sa)

Holidays

New Year's Day—January 1

Martin Luther King, Jr., Day—January 16*
(Third Monday in January)

Lincoln's Birthday—February 12

Washington's Birthday—February 22

Memorial Day—May 29*
(Last Monday in May)

Fourth of July/Independence Day—July 4

Labor Day—September 4*
(First Monday in September)

Columbus Day—October 9*
(Second Monday in October)

Thanksgiving—November 23*
(Last Thursday in November)

Christmas—December 25

*These dates are different from year to year.

1998

January 1998

S	M	T	W	T	F	S
				1	2	3
4	5	6	7	8	9	10
11	12	13	14	15	16	17
18	19	20	21	22	23	24
25	26	27	28	29	30	31

February 1998

S	M	T	W	T	F	S
1	2	3	4	5	6	7
8	9	10	11	12	13	14
15	16	17	18	19	20	21
22	23	24	25	26	27	28

March 1998

S	M	T	W	T	F	S
1	2	3	4	5	6	7
8	9	10	11	12	13	14
15	16	17	18	19	20	21
22	23	24	25	26	27	28
29	30	31				

April 1998

S	M	T	W	T	F	S
			1	2	3	4
5	6	7	8	9	10	11
12	13	14	15	16	17	18
19	20	21	22	23	24	25
26	27	28	29	30		

May 1998

S	M	T	W	T	F	S
					1	2
3	4	5	6	7	8	9
10	11	12	13	14	15	16
17	18	19	20	21	22	23
24	25	26	27	28	29	30
31						

June 1998

S	M	T	W	T	F	S
	1	2	3	4	5	6
7	8	9	10	11	12	13
14	15	16	17	18	19	20
21	22	23	24	25	26	27
28	29	30				

July 1998

S	M	T	W	T	F	S
			1	2	3	4
5	6	7	8	9	10	11
12	13	14	15	16	17	18
19	20	21	22	23	24	25
26	27	28	29	30	31	

August 1998

S	M	T	W	T	F	S
						1
2	3	4	5	6	7	8
9	10	11	12	13	14	15
16	17	18	19	20	21	22
23	24	25	26	27	28	29
30	31					

September 1998

S	M	T	W	T	F	S
		1	2	3	4	5
6	7	8	9	10	11	12
13	14	15	16	17	18	19
20	21	22	23	24	25	26
27	28	29	30			

October 1998

S	M	T	W	T	F	S
				1	2	3
4	5	6	7	8	9	10
11	12	13	14	15	16	17
18	19	20	21	22	23	24
25	26	27	28	29	30	31

November 1998

S	M	T	W	T	F	S
1	2	3	4	5	6	7
8	9	10	11	12	13	14
15	16	17	18	19	20	21
22	23	24	25	26	27	28
29	30					

December 1998

S	M	T	W	T	F	S
		1	2	3	4	5
6	7	8	9	10	11	12
13	14	15	16	17	18	19
20	21	22	23	24	25	26
27	28	29	30	31		

1999

January 1999

S	M	T	W	T	F	S
					1	2
3	4	5	6	7	8	9
10	11	12	13	14	15	16
17	18	19	20	21	22	23
24	25	26	27	28	29	30
31						

February 1999

S	M	T	W	T	F	S
	1	2	3	4	5	6
7	8	9	10	11	12	13
14	15	16	17	18	19	20
21	22	23	24	25	26	27
28						

March 1999

S	M	T	W	T	F	S
	1	2	3	4	5	6
7	8	9	10	11	12	13
14	15	16	17	18	19	20
21	22	23	24	25	26	27
28	29	30	31			

April 1999

S	M	T	W	T	F	S
				1	2	3
4	5	6	7	8	9	10
11	12	13	14	15	16	17
18	19	20	21	22	23	24
25	26	27	28	29	30	

May 1999

S	M	T	W	T	F	S
						1
2	3	4	5	6	7	8
9	10	11	12	13	14	15
16	17	18	19	20	21	22
23	24	25	26	27	28	29
30	31					

June 1999

S	M	T	W	T	F	S
		1	2	3	4	5
6	7	8	9	10	11	12
13	14	15	16	17	18	19
20	21	22	23	24	25	26
27	28	29	30			

July 1999

S	M	T	W	T	F	S
				1	2	3
4	5	6	7	8	9	10
11	12	13	14	15	16	17
18	19	20	21	22	23	24
25	26	27	28	29	30	31

August 1999

S	M	T	W	T	F	S
1	2	3	4	5	6	7
8	9	10	11	12	13	14
15	16	17	18	19	20	21
22	23	24	25	26	27	28
29	30	31				

September 1999

S	M	T	W	T	F	S
			1	2	3	4
5	6	7	8	9	10	11
12	13	14	15	16	17	18
19	20	21	22	23	24	25
26	27	28	29	30		

October 1999

S	M	T	W	T	F	S
					1	2
3	4	5	6	7	8	9
10	11	12	13	14	15	16
17	18	19	20	21	22	23
24	25	26	27	28	29	30
31						

November 1999

S	M	T	W	T	F	S
	1	2	3	4	5	6
7	8	9	10	11	12	13
14	15	16	17	18	19	20
21	22	23	24	25	26	27
28	29	30				

December 1999

S	M	T	W	T	F	S
			1	2	3	4
5	6	7	8	9	10	11
12	13	14	15	16	17	18
19	20	21	22	23	24	25
26	27	28	29	30	31	

Appendix 2
Cardinal and Ordinal Numbers

Cardinal Numbers		Ordinal Numbers
One	1	First
Two	2	Second
Three	3	Third
Four	4	Fourth
Five	5	Fifth
Six	6	Sixth
Seven	7	Seventh
Eight	8	Eighth
Nine	9	Ninth
Ten	10	Tenth
Eleven	11	Eleventh
Twelve	12	Twelfth
Thirteen	13	Thirteenth
Fourteen	14	Fourteenth
Fifteen	15	Fifteenth
Sixteen	16	Sixteenth
Seventeen	17	Seventeenth
Eighteen	18	Eighteenth
Nineteen	19	Nineteenth
Twenty	20	Twentieth
Twenty-One	21	Twenty-First
Twenty-Two	22	Twenty-Second
Twenty-Three	23	Twenty-Third
Twenty-Four	24	Twenty-Fourth
Twenty-Five	25	Twenty-Fifth
Twenty-Six	26	Twenty-Sixth
Twenty-Seven	27	Twenty-Seventh
Twenty-Eight	28	Twenty-Eighth
Twenty-Nine	29	Twenty-Ninth
Thirty	30	Thirtieth
Forty	40	Fortieth
Fifty	50	Fiftieth
Sixty	60	Sixtieth
Seventy	70	Seventieth
Eighty	80	Eightieth
Ninety	90	Ninetieth
One Hundred	100	One Hundredth

Appendix 3

Map of the World

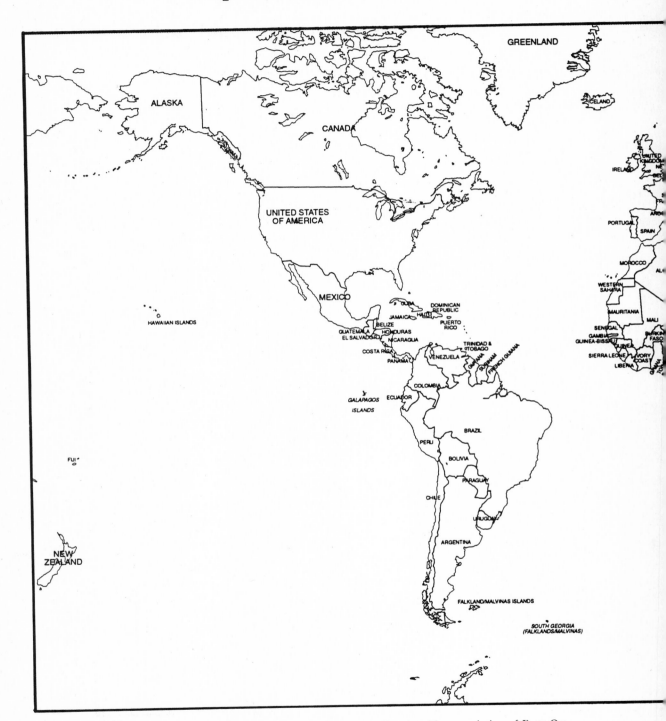

From *Maps On File*, copyright 1988 by Martin Greenwald Associates. Reprinted by permission of Facts On File, Inc., New York.

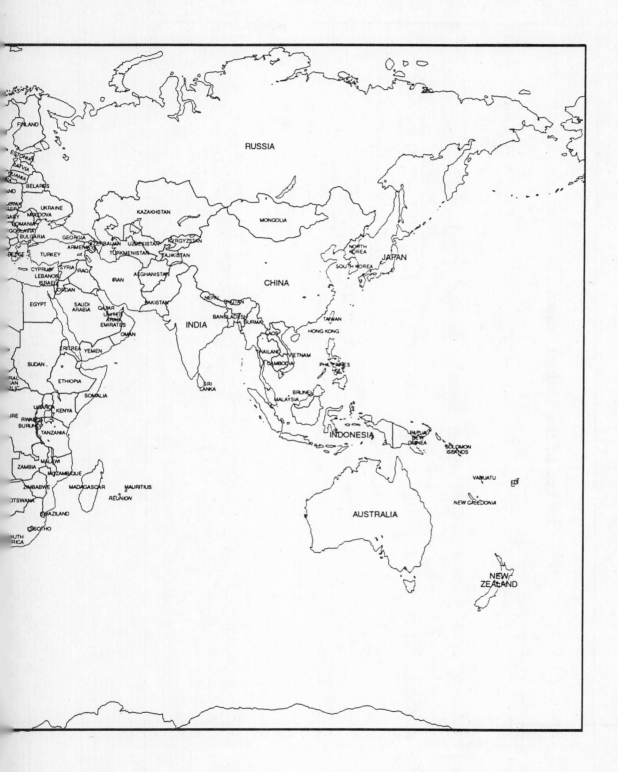

FINLAND
ESTONIA
LATVIA
LITHUANIA
BELARUS
UKRAINE
MOLDOVA
ROMANIA
BULGARIA
GEORGIA
ARMENIA
AZERBAIJAN
TURKEY
CYPRUS
SYRIA
LEBANON
ISRAEL
JORDAN
IRAQ
EGYPT
SAUDI
ARABIA
QATAR
UNITED
ARAB
EMIRATES
OMAN
ERITREA
YEMEN
SUDAN
ETHIOPIA
SOMALIA
UGANDA
KENYA
RWANDA
BURUNDI
TANZANIA
ZAMBIA
MALAWI
MOZAMBIQUE
ZIMBABWE
MADAGASCAR
MAURITIUS
RÉUNION
BOTSWANA
SWAZILAND
LESOTHO
SOUTH
AFRICA

RUSSIA

KAZAKHSTAN

MONGOLIA

UZBEKISTAN
KYRGYZSTAN
TURKMENISTAN
TAJIKISTAN

NORTH
KOREA
SOUTH KOREA
JAPAN

IRAN
AFGHANISTAN
PAKISTAN

CHINA

NEPAL
BHUTAN
INDIA
BANGLADESH
BURMA
TAIWAN

HONG KONG

LAOS
THAILAND
VIETNAM
CAMBODIA
PHILIPPINES

SRI
LANKA

BRUNEI
MALAYSIA

INDONESIA
PAPUA
NEW
GUINEA
SOLOMON
ISLANDS

VANUATU
FIJI
NEW CALEDONIA

AUSTRALIA

NEW
ZEALAND

Appendix 4

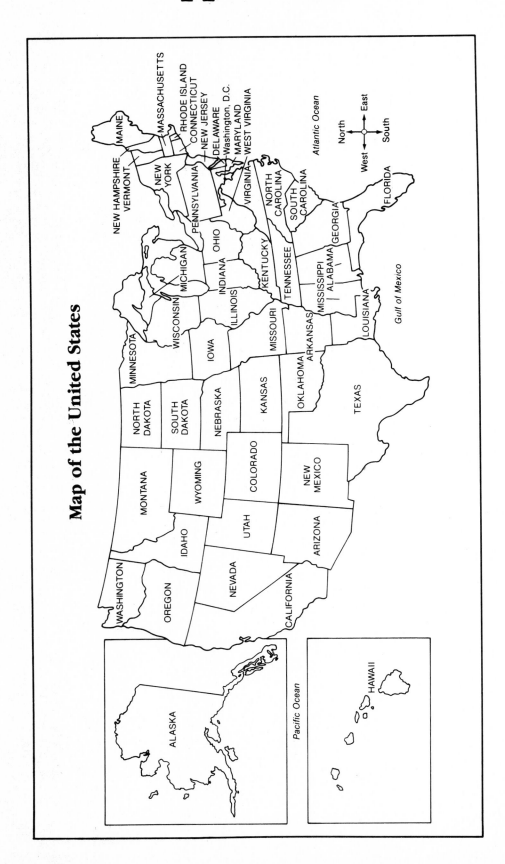

Map of the United States

Appendix 5

The States and Their Capitals

State	Capital	State	Capital
Alabama	Montgomery	Montana	Helena
Alaska	Juneau	Nebraska	Lincoln
Arizona	Phoenix	Nevada	Carson City
Arkansas	Little Rock	New Hampshire	Concord
California	Sacramento	New Jersey	Trenton
Colorado	Denver	New Mexico	Santa Fe
Connecticut	Hartford	New York	Albany
Delaware	Dover	North Carolina	Raleigh
Florida	Tallahassee	North Dakota	Bismarck
Georgia	Atlanta	Ohio	Columbus
Hawaii	Honolulu	Oklahoma	Oklahoma City
Idaho	Boise	Oregon	Salem
Illinois	Springfield	Pennsylvania	Harrisburg
Indiana	Indianapolis	Rhode Island	Providence
Iowa	Des Moines	South Carolina	Columbia
Kansas	Topeka	South Dakota	Pierre
Kentucky	Frankfort	Tennessee	Nashville
Louisiana	Baton Rouge	Texas	Austin
Maine	Augusta	Utah	Salt Lake City
Maryland	Annapolis	Vermont	Montpelier
Massachusetts	Boston	Virginia	Richmond
Michigan	Lansing	Washington	Olympia
Minnesota	St. Paul	West Virginia	Charleston
Mississippi	Jackson	Wisconsin	Madison
Missouri	Jefferson City	Wyoming	Cheyenne

Appendix 6

United States Presidents (and years served)

1. George Washington (1789-1797)
2. John Adams (1797-1801)
3. Thomas Jefferson (1801-1809)
4. James Madison (1809-1817)
5. James Monroe (1817-1825)
6. John Q. Adams (1825-1829)
7. Andrew Jackson (1829-1837)
8. Martin Van Buren (1837-1841)
9. William Harrison (1841)
10. John Tyler (1841-1845)
11. James Polk (1845-1849)
12. Zachary Taylor (1849-1850)
13. Millard Fillmore (1850-1853)
14. Franklin Pierce (1853-1857)
15. James Buchanan (1857-1861)
16. Abraham Lincoln (1861-1865)
17. Andrew Johnson (1865-1869)
18. Ulysses Grant (1869-1877)
19. Rutherford Hayes (1877-1881)
20. James Garfield (1881)
21. Chester Arthur (1881-1885)
22. Grover Cleveland (1885-1889)
23. Benjamin Harrison (1889-1893)
24. Grover Cleveland (1893-1897)
25. William McKinley (1897-1901)
26. Theodore Roosevelt (1901-1909)
27. William Taft (1909-1913)
28. Woodrow Wilson (1913-1921)
29. Warren Harding (1921-1923)
30. Calvin Coolidge (1923-1929)
31. Herbert Hoover (1929-1933)
32. Franklin Roosevelt (1933-1945)
33. Harry Truman (1945-1953)
34. Dwight Eisenhower (1953-1961)
35. John Kennedy (1961-1963)
36. Lyndon Johnson (1963-1969)
37. Richard Nixon (1969-1974)
38. Gerald Ford (1974-1977)
39. Jimmy Carter (1977-1981)
40. Ronald Reagan (1981-1989)
41. George Bush (1989 – 1993)
42. Bill Clinton (1993 –

Appendix 7

Star-Spangled Banner

Oh say, can you see, by the dawn's early light,
What so proudly we hailed at the twilight's last gleaming?
Whose broad stripes and bright stars, through the perilous fight,
O'er the ramparts we watched, were so gallantly streaming!
And the rockets' red glare, the bombs bursting in air,
Gave proof through the night that our flag was still there.
Oh say, does that star-spangled banner yet wave
O'er the land of the free and the home of the brave?

Pledge of Allegiance

I pledge allegiance to the flag of the United States of America
and to the republic for which it stands, one Nation under God,
indivisible, with liberty and justice for all.

Appendix 8

The Alphabet

Aa Bb Cc Dd Ee Ff Gg
Hh Ii Jj Kk Ll Mm Nn
Oo Pp Qq Rr Ss Tt Uu
Vv Ww Xx Yy Zz

A A	a a
B B	b b
C C	c c
D D	d d
E E	e e
F F	f f
G G	g g
H H	h h
I I	i i
J J	j j

K K	k k
L L	l l
M M	m m
N N	n n
O O	o o
P P	p p
Q Q	q q
R R	r r
S S	s s
T T	t t
U U	u u
V V	v v
W W	w w
X X	x x
Y Y	y y
Z Z	z z

U.S. Department of Justice
Immigration and Naturalization Service

Application to Adjust Status from Temporary to Permanent Resident
(Under Section 245 A of Public Law 99-603)

Please read instructions: fee will not be refunded.	Fee Stamp
INS Use: Bar Code	
SAMPLE	
Address Label	
(Place adhesive address label here from booklet **or** fill in name and address, and A 90 million file number in appropriate blocks.)	Applicant's File No. A - 9 _ _ _ _ _ _ _

1. **Family Name** *(Last Name in CAPITAL Letters) (See instructions) (First Name) (Middle Name)*	2. Sex ☐ Male ☐ Female
3. **Name as it appears** on Temporary Resident Card *(I-688)* if different from above.	4. Phone No.'s *(Include Area Codes)* Home: Work:

5. **Reason for difference in name** *(See instructions)*

	(Apt. No.)	(City)	(State)	(Zip Code)
6. Home Address *(No. and Street)*				
7. Mailing Address *(if different)*				

8. Place of Birth *(City or Town)*	*(County, Province or State)* *(Country)*	9. Date of Birth *(Month/Day/Year)*
10. **Your Mother's First Name**	11. **Your Father's First Name**	12. Enter your Social Security Number _ _ _ - _ _ - _ _ _ _

13. **Absences from the United States since becoming a Temporary Resident Alien.** *(List most recent first.) (If you have a single absence in excess of 30 days or the total of all your absences exceeds 90 days, explain and attach any relevant information).*

Country	Purpose of Trip	From *(Month/Day/Year)*	To *(Month/Day/Year)*	Total Days Absent

14. **When applying for temporary resident alien status, I**
☐ did ☐ did not submit a medical examination form (I-693) with my application that included a serologic (blood) test for human immunodeficiency virus (HIV) infection. *(If you did not, submit a medical examination form (I-693) with this application that includes a serologic test for HIV.)*

15. **Since becoming a temporary resident alien, I**
☐ have ☐ have not been arrested, convicted or confined in a prison. *(If you have, provide the date(s), place(s), specific charge(s) and attach any relevant information.)*

16. **Since becoming a temporary resident alien, I**
☐ have ☐ have not been the beneficiary of a pardon, amnesty (other than legalization), rehabilitation decree, other act of clemency or similar action. *(If you have, explain and attach any relevant documentation.)*

17. **Since becoming a temporary resident alien, I**
☐ have ☐ have not received public assistance from any source, including but not limited to, the United States Government, any state, county, city or municipality. *(If you have, explain, including the name(s) and Social Security Number(s) used and attach any relevant information.)*

Form I-698 (08/10/88) Page 1

18. Concerning the requirement of minimal understanding of ordinary English and a knowledge and understanding of the history and government of the United States: (*Check appropriate block under Section A or B.*)

A. I will satisfy these requirements by;
- ☐ Examination at the time of interview for permanent residence.
- ☐ Satisfactorily pursuing a course of study recognized by the Attorney General.

B. I have satisfied these requirements by;
- ☐ Having satisfactorily pursued a course of study recognized by the Attorney General (*please attach appropriate documentation*).
- ☐ Exemption, in that I am 65 years of age or older, under the age of 16, or I am physically unable to comply. (*If physically unable to comply, explain and attach relevant documentation.*)

SAMPLE

---

19. Applicants for status as Permanent Residents must establish that they are not excludable from the United States under the following provisions of section 212 of the INA. An applicant who is excludable under a provision of section 212 (a) which may not be waived is ineligible for permanent resident status. An applicant who is excludable under a provision of section 212 (a) which may be waived may, if otherwise eligible, be granted permanent resident status, if an application for waiver on form I-690 is filed and approved.

A. Grounds for exclusion which *may not be waived:*
- Listed by paragraph number of section 212 (a);

____ (9) Aliens who have committed or who have been convicted of a crime involving moral turpitude (does not include minor traffic violations).
____ (10) Aliens who have been convicted of two or more offenses for which the aggregate sentences to confinement actually imposed were five years or more.
____ (15) Aliens likely to become a public charge.
____ (23) Aliens who have been convicted of a violation of any law or regulation relating to narcotic drugs or marihuana, or who have been illicit traffickers in narcotic drugs or marihuana.
____ (27) Aliens who intend to engage in activities prejudicial to the national interests or unlawful activities of a subversive nature.
____ (28) Aliens who are or at any time have been anarchists, or members of or affiliated with any Communist or other totalitarian party, including any subdivision or affiliate thereof.
____ (29) Aliens who have advocated or taught, either by personal utterance, or by means of any written matter, or through affiliation with an organization:
  1) Opposition to organized government;
  2) The overthrow of government by force or violence;
  3) The assaulting or killing of government officials because of their official character;
  4) The unlawful destruction of property;
  5) Sabotage; or,
  6) The doctrines of world communism, or the establishment of a totalitarian dictatorship in the United States.
____ (33) Aliens who, during the period beginning on March 23, 1933, and ending on May 8, 1945, under the direction of, and in association with:
  1) The Nazi government in Germany;
  2) Any government in any area occupied by the military forces of the Nazi government in Germany;
  3) Any government established with the assistance or cooperation of the Nazi government of Germany;
  4) Any government which was an ally of the Nazi government of Germany;
  ordered, incited, assisted or otherwise participated in the persecution of any person because of race, religion, national origin, or political opinion.
- Provisions of 212 (e):
____ Aliens who at any time were exchange visitors subject to the two-year foreign residence requirement unless the requirement has been satisfied or waived pursuant to the provisions of section 212 (e) of the Act. (Does not apply to the Extended Voluntary Departure (EVD) class of temporary resident aliens).

Do any of the above classes apply to you?
☐ No ☐ Yes (*If "Yes", attach an explanation, and any relevant documentation. Place mark (X) on line before ground(s) of exclusion.*)

B. Grounds for exclusion which *may be waived:*
- Listed by paragraph number of section 212 (a);

____ (1) Aliens who are mentally retarded.
____ (2) Aliens who are insane.
____ (3) Aliens who have suffered one or more attacks of insanity.
____ (4) Aliens afflicted with psychopathic personality, sexual deviation, or a mental defect.
____ (5) Aliens who are narcotic drug addicts or chronic alcoholics.
____ (6) Aliens who are afflicted with any dangerous contagious disease.
____ (7) Aliens who have a physical defect, disease or disability affecting their ability to earn a living.
____ (8) Aliens who are paupers, professional beggars or vagrants.
____ (11) Aliens who are polygamists or advocate polygamy.
____ (12) Aliens who are prostitutes or former prostitutes, or who have procured or attempted to procure or to import, prostitutes or persons for the purpose of prostitution or for any other immoral purpose, or aliens coming to the United States to engage in any other unlawful commercialized vice, whether or not related to prostitution.
____ (13) Aliens coming to the United States to engage in any immoral sexual act.
____ (16) Aliens who have been excluded from admission and deported and who again seek admission within one year from the date of such deportation.
____ (17) Aliens who have been arrested and deported and who reentered the United States within five years from the date of deportation.
____ (19) Aliens who have procured or have attempted to procure a visa or other documentation by fraud, or by willfully misrepresenting a material fact.
____ (22) Aliens who have applied for exemption or discharge from training or service in the Armed Forces of the United States on the ground of alienage and who have been relieved or discharged from such training or service.
____ (31) Aliens who at any time shall have, knowingly and for gain, encouraged, induced, assisted, abetted, or aided any other alien to enter or to try to enter the United States in violation of law.

Do any of the above classes apply to you?
☐ No ☐ Yes (*If "Yes", attach an explanation, and any relevant documentation and submit Form I-690. Place mark (X) on line before ground(s) of exclusion.*)

---

20. If your native alphabet is other than Roman letters, write your name in your native alphabet.	21. Language of native alphabet
22. Signature of Applicant - *I CERTIFY*, under penalty of perjury under the laws of the United States of America that the foregoing is true and correct. I hereby consent and authorize the Service to verify the information provided, and to conduct record checks pertinent to this application.	23. Date (*Month/Day/Year*)
24. Signature of person preparing form, if other than applicant. I DECLARE that this document was prepared by me at the request of the applicant and is based on all information of which I have any knowledge.	25. Date (*Month/Day/Year*)
26. Name and Address of person preparing form, if **other than applicant** (*type or print*).	27. Occupation

Page 2

CONTEMPORARY'S
Look at the U.S. Series

Contemporary Books is pleased to present an ESL/civics series based on the content of the federal citizenship texts.

This unique, innovative program teaches the basics of American history and government while reinforcing the English language skills of listening, speaking, reading, and writing. In addition to the content-based lessons in the student texts, extra listening, speaking, and writing practice is provided in activity-oriented teacher's guides.

Look at the U.S. is a multi-level program to ensure that civics concepts are learned at different levels of English ability. This flexible series can be used in amnesty programs, in ESL classrooms, and for citizenship preparation.

Program Components

Three Student Texts

Literacy Level
   preliterate & beginning
Book 1
   high beginning & low intermediate
Book 2
   intermediate & above

Two Teacher's Guides

Literacy Level
Books 1 & 2

Look at the U.S.—Literacy Level

Content

Personal Identification
Cities, States, and Countries
American History Through
   Holidays
People and Places to Know
American Symbols

Special Features

U.S. and World Maps
U.S. Presidents
States and Capitals
Pledge of Allegiance and the
   "Star-Spangled Banner"
Sample Permanent Residency Form

CB

CONTEMPORARY BOOKS

a division of NTC/CONTEMPORARY PUBLISHING GROUP

ISBN: 0-8092-4329-6

9 780809 243297

ISBN 0-8092-4329-6

90000

CONTEMPORARY'S
LOOK AT THE U.S.

An ESL/Civics Series
Based on the Federal Citizenship Texts

Teacher's Guide–Literacy Level